Distance Education, Electronic Networking, and School Policy

by
Tom Clark
and
David Else

ISBN 0-87367-641-6

Bloomington, Indiana

This fastback is sponsored by the University of Kentucky Chapter of Phi Delta Kappa International and the University of Kentucky Department of Administration and Supervision in the College of Education, which made a generous contribution toward publication costs.

This fastback is sponsored to commemorate the 75th anniversary of the University of Kentucky College of Education and the 70th anniversary of the University of Kentucky Chapter of Phi Delta Kappa International. The College of Education provides statewide leadership in technology research and delivery of academic programs through distance education. The Department of Administration and Supervision has a special interest in distance learning. In 1990 this department began one of the first doctoral programs in the country using interactive video classes. Technology for distance learning gives educators throughout Kentucky access to the programs of the University of Kentucky and College of Education.

Table of Contents

Introduction

Distance education and electronic networking affect school policy at all levels. Educators everywhere are being called on to make and deal with new policies related to the who's, how's, and why's of new electronic communications media. And the policy demands are growing as rapidly as the proliferation of distance education and electronic networking technologies. In Iowa, for example, more than 400 schools will have video and Internet connections through the statewide Iowa Communications Network by the year 2001. Local, regional, and state networks are being created across the country, as schools rush to take advantage of the "information highway." Access to discounts on telecommunications services using the FCC's "E-Rate" can only accelerate this trend.

School administrators have been dealing with distance education policy issues in relation to independent study and satellite courses for many years, but such issues usually have not been central in school policy. Today policy decisions must be made at every level in order for a complete regional or statewide distance education system or electronic network to function effectively. This rapid proliferation is bringing these policy matters to the forefront. And the concepts of distributed learning, learning communities, and virtual schools are creating new policy issues for the future.

In this fastback we focus on policy issues that schools encounter as they become involved with distance education and electronic networking. Our intention is to create a brief resource guide for school administrators, teachers, policy makers, and others interested in policy issues of this sort.

We believe that educators, school board members, and others who shape policy and deal with the consequences of policy need clear information about new distance education and electronic networking issues in order to compete effectively for resources, participate meaningfully in consortia, and competently manage distance education and related technologies in their institutions. To illustrate this need we recount the following case.

"E-Rate" Challenges

Perhaps no federal action has had a more galvanizing effect on K-12 and library technology planning than the Education Rate, or "E-Rate," resulting from the federal Telecommunications Act of 1996.

Under the act the Federal Communications Commission (FCC) is mandated to develop telecommunications service discount mechanisms for schools, libraries, and rural health facilities. It adopted the report of a special board in May 1997 and established organizations, including the Schools and Libraries Corporation (SLC), to administer funding of 20% to 90% discounts beginning on 1 January 1998.

This funding, originally capped at $2.25 billion annually, comes from the Universal Service Fund contributions required of telephone companies. E-Rate discounts are on a sliding scale based on rurality and poverty levels. School administrators nationwide have shown an ability to move rapidly on technology issues in their work to qualify for the E-Rate discounts. But faced with a 75-day window for "first-come, first-served" applications for 1998 funding, state agencies have been hard pressed to provide sufficient technical assistance to local administrators in fulfilling E-Rate requirements. Applicants have needed to develop comprehensive, cost-effective technology plans and technology inventories or to enhance existing plans to include such items as planned and existing Internet connectivity, wiring and electrical capacity, and maintenance contracts. They have had to prepare for implementation of specific staff development and technology integration, as described in their technology plans. And often they have had to develop new planning and budgeting approaches for the E-Rate, because services to be discounted are to be contracted on a calendar year, rather than a federal fiscal year or school year basis.

Applicants also have needed to establish effective bidding procedures for services, with relatively short deadlines, to complete the application process. The result has been a need for rapid planning and decision making by school administrators. In fact, many administrators completed their local planning from draft E-Rate program requirements, prior to issuance of approved forms, before the beginning of the 75-day "window" in order to meet the need to issue a request for proposals and complete the bidding process before the window closed.

Some of the challenges presented by the E-Rate may reflect a lack of awareness on the part of the FCC of standard operating procedures of schools. Seeking to encourage competition among providers, the FCC originally adopted a calendar year-to-year approach. But schools usually follow a federal fiscal year approach, and they usually have enacted multi-year contracts for telecommunications services. On 13 June 1998 the FCC enacted important changes in the E-Rate. They moved from a calendar year to a fiscal year, which educators liked; but in response to industry and congressional criticism, they also effectively scaled back the cap on maximum funding about 57%, from $2.25 billion to $1.4 billion annually.

In spite of the challenges, and based on the effects of special tariffs on K-12 networking in some states, the FCC's E-Rate program is expected to have a positive effect on distance education and networking. A survey of state departments of education for the State Networking Report (Mayer et al. 1997) showed that in states with special tariffs, more school districts, teachers, and students tended to have network access. State contacts in a large majority of states (46 of 50, or 92%) also characterized the E-Rate as having a "positive impact" on K-12 network development.

Because telecommunications services and connections are estimated to constitute only 11% or less of total costs of networking, the potential effect of the E-Rate must be kept in perspective. Nevertheless, the E-Rate illustrates the widespread effects that policy can have on distance education and electronic networking.

Distance Education and Electronic Networking

Following is an overview of the technologies in question and some of their applications. For starters, *distance education,* also called *distance learning* or *distance teaching,* is teaching and learning in which "a majority of the instruction occurs while educator and learner are at a distance from one another" (Verduin and Clark 1991). Holznagel and Olson also define distance education as "a system of instruction which makes use of one or more educational technologies," where educational technology is defined as "a collection of devices, media and techniques which can be used for instruction" (1990, p. 2).

Distance education delivery systems are used in a wide range of school activities. We are interested here primarily in those forms of distance education that involve the use of telecommunications, computers, and electronic networking.

Electronic networking refers to the interconnection of computers and other electronic devices in various kinds of networks. Networks can range from the local area networks (LANs) within individual computer labs or administrative offices to campus- or districtwide area networks (WANs), statewide educational telecommunications networks, and the global "network of networks," the Internet.

Electronic networks often are part of distance learning delivery systems. However, their potential use in schools is far broader. Schools are finding that electronic networking can play an important role in technologically integrating the curriculum and meeting education reform goals, as well as in administrative functions, school library information systems, and other areas critical to school effectiveness. But in this fastback we focus on the use of these technologies for learning, rather than for administration.

New Ways of Thinking

Many educators, parents, and students are excited about the new instructional possibilities that can result from the growth in electronic networking. In distributed learning, as envisioned by Dede (1996), "knowledge webs complement teachers, tests, libraries, and archives as sources of information; interactions in virtual communities complement face-to-face relationships in classrooms; and experiences in synthetic environments extend learning-by-doing in real world settings." Whereas classroom-based distance education in many ways replicates traditional classroom teaching across barriers of time and space, distributed learning offers new challenges for education policy makers already dealing with issues arising from "synchronous" methods, such as two-way video. Norris (1997) envisions "knowledge age" learning enterprises transformed by distributed learning.

Another result of electronic networking and distance education is that schools become part of a larger learning community. Networking schools and integrating technology is not sufficient for long-term success. Public schools that join with government and business in local learning communities will stand a much better chance of sustained public support and funding for their networking efforts. They also will keep a larger share of the local education market — not a small concern in a time of high interest in privatization of public education.

The challenge to think in new ways about distance education and electronic communications media and networking has a long history in the fastback series, and we would be remiss not to point out some of the titles to which readers might wish to refer. These include: 366 *Technology in Rural Education*, an excellent introduction for the rural educator; 335 *Using Telecommunications in Middle School Reading*; 356 *Using Computer Technology to Create a Global Classroom*; and, most recently, 438 *Technological Collaborations: K-12 and Higher Education*; 439 *Distance Education and Tomorrow's Schools*; and 440 *Distance Education and Teacher Education at Armstrong Atlantic State University*. Distance learning also is becoming an integral part of subfields in education, as evidenced in 409 *Trends Shaping the Future of Special Education* and in 406 *Teacher Study Groups for Professional Development*.

Forms of Distance Education

The use of distance education in schools is growing. A recent annual federal study found that 22% of all public schools used advanced telecommunications for distance education, including 19% of elementary schools and 33% of secondary schools (Heaviside et al. 1997). The development of electronic networking capabilities in K-12 education is increasing at an even faster pace. About 64% of all public schools had Internet access in fall 1996, a four-fold increase over only a few years. Following are descriptions of several forms of distance education.

Independent study is the oldest form of distance education and still enrolls more K-12 students than other forms of distance learning. For example, the University of Nebraska-Lincoln's Independent Study High School currently enrolls nearly 14,000 students annually, more than a third of them in the full diploma program. A wide variety of media can be used in independent study, including CD-ROMs, videodiscs, videotapes, and audiotapes. The use of electronic networking for communication between teachers and learners is blurring the distinction between independent study and distributed learning. State education agencies usually have a contact person for approval and referral to accredited providers, and some have their own independent study programs. Major providers of K-12 independent study include a number of state universities.

Broadcast and cable television are used by many organizations to provide courses, supplemental and enrichment programming, and staff development. Broadcast television courses, called telecourses, can be viewed live or on videotape by learners in their homes. But most broadcast instructional television programming is noninteractive and intended for videotape use during the school day. Many schools have their own cable-TV community learning systems, used for instructional and interactive programming for students and community members. About three-quarters of all schools have access to cable television, and more than 90% have access to open broadcast programming. Cable TV penetration should grow under the Cable in the Classroom program, especially with availability of telecommunications discounts for schools. Providers include PBS K-12 Learning Services and Cable in the Classroom.

One-way video, two-way audio is live television delivered by satellite or broadcast to schools, with use of the telephone for interaction. A number of organizations offer enrichment, coursework, and staff development by this method. A facilitator or monitor is required, who may be a certified teacher or a classroom aide, depending on state requirements. About one-fifth of schools have access to satellite videoconferencing technology, with higher percentages in rural states. Providers work with specific groups of states, often where their instructors are certified or courses are approved. Major providers include StarNet (previously TI-IN), ASTS, MCET and SERC.

Video-only satellite is a form used by a number of services to provide supplemental and enrichment programs and staff development. This method uses television programs delivered by satellite without telephone interaction. Channel One, paid for through commercial advertising, reaches some 8 million students through about 12,000 satellite dishes installed in schools nationwide (Levine 1997). Other providers include CNN Newsroom, NASA, NOAA, and SCOLA.

Two-way video, two-way audio is live television with both origination site and participating sites having video origination capabilities, usually along with dedicated audio. Technologies for two-way video include the regular phone line, cable, microwave, and fiber optics, with transmission speeds from a few frames per second through broadcast-quality full motion. States with large-scale, two-way video networks include Iowa, North Carolina, and Georgia. Many hundreds of smaller networks connect schools and districts, with statewide interconnections planned or under way.

Computer-based media are commonly used to supplement conventional instruction. Computer media also have a growing role in independent study and multimedia approaches to distance education. CD-ROM is the fastest growing educational technology because it incorporates many multimedia computers and thus decreases software cost. Currently, about 98% of schools own computers, while 85% own multimedia computers. More than half have computers with CD-ROM drives. Use of local area networks (LANs) for sharing computer materials is growing, with about four in 10 schools currently using LANs in instruction.

Computer-mediated communication is used by a number of organizations to offer supplementary instruction, database access, bulletin boards, and discussion groups through dial-up connections. Most of these services are migrating to web-based interfaces for use by means of local high-speed connections to the Internet. They provide additional sources of information to complement classroom and school libraries.

The Internet is the information highway. For the foreseeable future, the World Wide Web, the Internet's key component, is likely to serve as an umbrella technology uniting distance education media for distributed learning. Applications such as desktop video allow low-cost individual videoconferencing between computers on the Internet. Statewide computer networks with combined audio, video, and data capabilities are replacing earlier dial-up demonstration projects and connecting small regional video networks. Many nonprofit consortia are forming, locally to globally, to use the Internet to provide educational opportunities. National providers include FrEdMail, K12 Net, NASA Spacelink, and World Classroom.

Virtual schooling is the next wave. Some universities now offer complete K-12 courses by "electronic correspondence study," and K-12 "virtual schools" offering complete instructional programs are under development. An example is the University of Nebraska's CLASS (Communication, Learning, Assessment in a Student-centered System), a web-based course environment. Scheduled for completion in 2001, CLASS will offer an entire high school diploma sequence. Van Horn (1997) suggests a future where students might use "learning pods" distributed among public and private agencies in a larger learning community.

Policy Issues and Roles

A flurry of federal and state legislation, regulation, and direct assistance in the last few years has been aimed at linking schools and libraries to the information highway. The rush to network has created both challenges and opportunities for educators. Following is a summary of the federal, state, and local roles related to policy issues arising from this endeavor.

Federal Role

The general policy role of the federal government has remained unchanged over time, though the emphases have changed under different guiding philosophies. For the most part, federal policy makers are concerned with research, development, dissemination, coordination, advocacy, and legislation. The federal government has only limited direct control over state and local policy. However, federal mandates and incentives can create at least the appearance of reform at the state and local level.

In the last few years, federal policy on distance learning has become focused largely on planning for technology access and integration into the curriculum in support of systemic education reform. We will say more about the evolution of federal initiatives later.

State Role

States are involved in accountability, certification, equity, funding, and quality issues. States mandate standards-based education reforms, often in reaction to standards-based federal initiatives that carry requirements for pass-through funding. They also provide varying amounts of professional development and technical assistance to support these standards and initiatives.

Prior to the growth of distance learning and electronic networking in the 1980s, state policies on school technology were considerably simpler. State education agencies usually had staff for dealing with computers in schools and, later, with technology coordination. With the growth of telecommunications-based distance learning and then the explosion of electronic networking, a number of additional state agencies became involved in distance learning policy.

The role of the state in distance learning and electronic networking can vary from design and implementation of a statewide network with heavy technical assistance to a focus on providing information and resources to support school and district planning. Most states are now addressing equity and access problems through technology, partly through investments in statewide electronic networks and distance learning programs. Some states are providing substantial technical assistance, but most provide only limited funding for staff development, maintenance, upgrades, and technical support. Most states consider these to be district-level responsibilities.

Key state issues for distance learning and electronic networking include system planning, funding, equity and access, and certification. Still on the horizon are issues such as "seat time," which must be addressed if "virtual schooling" approaches are to be mainstreamed.

Local Role

Principals typically exercise management, mediation, and leadership in their schools (Lee, Bryk, and Smith 1993). They coordinate instructional guidance to teachers, establish and enforce building rules and policies, and supervise staff development and evaluation. They also facilitate external communication and communicate about policy decisions internally. Finally, they shape and define formal and informal school goals and provide guidance and supervision in instruction.

It is important for district, regional, and state-level policy makers to take the views of school building administrators into account in reaching distance education policy determinations that will affect the use of communications networks by schools. Local, building-level administrators deal on a day-to-day basis with issues critical to widespread implementation, such as coordination, supervision, and course sharing.

District administrators usually provide facility and strategic planning, administrative direction, and instructional guidance, including staff development, curriculum guidelines and materials, supervision, and assessment. School districts often have moved to meet their instructional needs through distance learning and networking prior to the creation of statewide networks, because they are driven by local situations and circumstances or the need to meet state curriculum mandates.

Local districts (central office) do not figure prominently in contemporary school reform efforts, which are centered at the state level, on one hand, and the local, individual school level, on the other hand (Spillane 1996). However, districts are important in instructional policy because of their major role in providing instructional guidance to schools. In order to support high standards, state-level policy makers strengthen state instructional policies for teachers. This leads to more district-level instructional policy making and often to duplication and unfocused guidance. Some critics would conclude that state-level policy makers should work with districts, rather than ignoring them on these issues.

Emerging Issues

A number of issues are emerging with the proliferation of distance education and electronic networking. Most prominent among them are access and equity.

Thirty-seven of 40 states (92.5%) replying to England's (1991) survey believed that distance education systems can provide a viable alternative for states that must address funding-equity issues among districts.

Based on a survey of southeastern states, Jones (1994) found that most were addressing equity and access problems through technology, partly through investments in the statewide electronic networks and distance education programs. However, progress in the development of distance education and electronic networking has been extremely uneven from state to state, related to such factors as rural/urban status, poverty, and ethnicity. Findings about access and equity can be found in the Educational Testing Service report, *Computers and Classrooms* (Coley et al. 1997), which reviewed a number of recent national surveys and studies.

Access to multimedia computers and the Internet in 100% of U.S. classrooms is still a distant goal. About 64% of all public schools have access to the Internet, but only 14% of classrooms have Internet access. Multimedia computer access varies greatly from state to state, with statewide student-to-multimedia computer ratios ranging from 8.5:1 to more than 50:1, with an average of 24:1. The optimal ratio is 5:1.

Universal teacher access to technology training also is a goal. About 20% of teachers used advanced telecommunications in fall 1996. About 13% of teachers took mandated technology training, while 31% received incentives to participate in such training.

Rural schools make more use of advanced telecommunications for distance learning than do other schools (29% as opposed to 22% of all schools), especially satellite-based learning. However, in states without free universal dial-up access for districts, urban school districts are approximately three times more likely than rural school districts to have such access.

Access in high-minority and high-poverty schools is limited. Only 17% of these schools used advanced telecommunications for distance learning. However, with the exception of high-minority schools, poorer schools had better access than wealthier schools to satellite technology. Gains in computing resources achieved in previous years by high-poverty schools through Title I have not continued in this direction.

The National Center for Education Statistics also studied private school technology use in fall 1995 (NCES 1997). Percentages of public and private schools with computers were very similar, but private schools lagged behind in multimedia computers. About one in four private schools had Internet access in fall 1995, compared to 50% of public schools. Only 5% of classrooms in private schools had Internet access, compared to 9% in public schools.

Technology access and use in schools is still far from the "four pillars" goals of universal access to hardware, content, professional development, and connectivity that are essential for technology literacy. The CEO Forum on Education and Technology (1997) estimates that only 3% of schools currently provide a "Target Tech" technology-rich environment needed for true technology literacy. However, the forum also acknowledges that there are no national evaluations under way using tools that actually measure the effects of technology integration on learning progress, quality of content, or levels and kinds of staff development. Evaluating technology integration on a nationwide basis would be a formidable task.

On average, in states surveyed in *The State Networking Report* (Mayer et al. 1997), 50% of K-12 educators and 10% of students were reported to have network access. Yet only 40% of those with network access actually used it. Fully networking schools will have limited usefulness if teachers do not decide to integrate technology into their everyday work. Well-planned professional development opportunities, not mandated use, is key.

Although access and equity are major issues, several other issues are clamoring for attention, including:

Certification. A majority of states require teacher certification for distance instructors. However, it does not appear likely that the use of telecommunications and technology will facilitate a movement toward a national teacher certification program, in spite of some of the advantages that might accrue from such a move.

Scheduling. Among the many challenges associated with distance education is scheduling. Block scheduling stands out as an instructional innovation that may play a role in building the school of the future, which may further challenge distance education. Distance learning that relies on live ("real-time") classroom instruction, whether satellite-based or network-based, generally follows traditional scheduling patterns.

Funding. Finding ways to finance distance education and electronic networking is a major problem for schools. For example, estimates of the cost of putting all U.S. schools and classrooms on the Internet range from $50 billion to $100 billion. The Pelavin Research Institute (1997) offers a wide variety of specific funding strategies for school districts, but it is unlikely that all districts will be able to find a funding strategy that works.

Local control. There is considerable controversy over the effect of federal policy on local control of schools. The Republican congressional leadership has focused on methods of enhancing local control and limiting the influence of the federal government in education reform, has slowed adoption of national testing standards, and has sought to allot education block grants directly to school districts without reporting requirements. State and federal technical assistance may be significantly reduced in this scenario.

School Principals and the Policy Issues

Without the support of superintendents and principals, education reform efforts cannot be implemented successfully. They are key players in technology integration efforts, including those involving large-scale use of distance education. But what about principals in particular?

In 1996 we studied distance education and electronic networking policy issues by surveying Iowa principals whose high schools were connected to the Iowa Communications Network (Clark and Else 1998). An ICN "point of presence" and video classroom site will be established in at least one high school in each of Iowa's 384 public school districts by June 2000. Internet connectivity using the ICN also is available to institutions obtaining a "point of presence" and video classroom, and most have installed such connections. The results of this survey suggest that building administrators whose schools have recently connected with other schools in the region or state through educational networks may face substantial challenges related to coordination and other issues.

Eighty percent or more of principals responding to this survey agreed that the following 10 issues were important for "effective use of the ICN."

1. Teacher/administrator video classroom training.
2. Common semesters.
3. Teacher/administrator Internet training.
4. Matching ICN courses with the best available sites.
5. Common bell schedules.
6. Supervision, proctoring, after-hours staffing.
7. Internet acceptable-use policy.
8. Technical support for hardware, software, network usage.
9. Student Internet training.
10. School/ICN video classroom closings, cancellations.

In addition, the respondents also indicated that most of the policy issues were not being addressed as adequately as they should be. In examining these results, we made several observations in a range of categories:

Coordination. The principals who responded to our survey indicated that coordination with external parties required the most action for networks to be used effectively. Difficulties establishing a common schedule with other schools for ICN video classroom courses were mentioned by many respondents, including several who specifically mentioned difficulties with block scheduling. Substantial numbers mentioned internal scheduling difficulties at their schools related to ICN use and difficulties in sharing course information or coordinating with other schools. Network scheduling also turned out to be more complicated for local decision makers than anyone had anticipated.

Technology training. Clearly, training teachers and administrators to use ICN video classrooms and the Internet were very important issues for respondents, while student Internet training was seen as moderately important. Principals supported staff development for system use early in the process, sharing the sentiment of one respondent that this was crucial to "getting the room used."

Staffing. Issues of staffing and supervision were frequently cited by principals, who often directly or indirectly indicated their own increased time commitment and responsibility. For example, a respondent wrote, "One more responsibility of the principal in a lot of cases — especially when outsiders use the system"; another said, "It does take a lot of someone's time to make sure the building is open and the room is available for installation of equipment, etc."

Facilities and technical support. Some respondents cited construction delays or equipment problems, but most frequently their construction-related responses concerned decisions related to room installation. Some gave highly specific advice for school administrators planning new ICN rooms, such as "placement of room to limit building access for ICN room usage" and "access to restroom during non-school hours."

Leadership issues. Leadership activities to obtain support, such as "visioning" or strategic planning, were named as key issues by a number of respondents. For example, one principal gave as a key issue, "Getting teachers, parents, and students excited about the possibilities. Sharing the vision and having a positive experience right away." Another was more blunt, calling the key issue " 'selling' the ICN to instructional staff."

Teacher rewards. Teacher rewards were an important issue for the future, according to the responding principals, though the rewards issue was not as pressing as coordination issues, staffing, or teacher video training. Teacher job security was seen as a "non-issue" by a majority of respondents.

Support for technology use. About 93% of responding principals said their school administration supported the use of distance education, but significantly fewer (72%) agreed that their school's teachers supported distance education. Practically all felt that both teachers and administrators supported Internet use.

Larger and smaller schools. Monk (1986) found that secondary schools with enrollments under 480 had difficulty offering a comprehensive curriculum. We decided that comparing the perceptions of respondents whose high schools had smaller (less than 400 students) and larger (400+) enrollments might yield some interesting results. We found that principals of larger schools rated the importance of student video training less highly than did principals of smaller schools. Principals of smaller schools were less concerned about common bell schedules and semesters than were larger-school principals. Smaller-school principals were more likely to see current access to the Internet and to ICN interactive television courses as adequate and more likely to see staffing for these activities as adequate.

In conclusion, it seems clear that early planning for coordination of courses and curricula needs to be promoted by states through dissemination of models, funding of institutes, providing Internet resources, and other methods. The staffing issues of school administrators also should be addressed, as should rural-urban differences in perceptions. Strategies are needed to promote peer-to-peer networking between schools that use common calendars and schedules and to coordinate courses and curricula between schools with dissimilar calendars or schedules.

Federal Actions on Technology and Reform

Distance education and electronic networking still play a limited role in education reform. With funding assistance and agendas coming from several different federal agencies and from multiple initiatives within the U.S. Department of Education, state and local educators may well see the guidance provided from the federal level as diffuse, sometimes even contradictory. However, the federal government has been able to set the agenda for technology integration in many ways. While implementation is in state and local hands, it is worthwhile to examine some of the notable federal actions.

In fact, distance education and electronic networking have become the primary vehicles for many federally funded education reform efforts. At least eight federal agencies have grant programs that support distance education or electronic networking in schools (Krebs 1996), including the Department of Education. Recent federal initiatives and programs providing significant funding and direction for K-12 networking and distance learning include:

Star Schools. Since 1988 the U.S. Department of Education has funded six cycles of two-year statewide and multistate projects under the Star Schools Program Assistance Act, as authorized under Title I of the Elementary and Secondary Education Act (ESEA), to serve underserved populations through distance education technologies.

National Information Infrastructure. A 1992 initiative was the National Information Infrastructure (NII), conceived as a seamless web of communication networks, computers, databases, and consumer electronics, which would lead to an "information revolution" to transform society. The Department of Education sought priority for education policy issues, such as lifelong learning, on the NII agenda (Ramirez and Bell 1994) and positioned itself for large-scale funding through related initiatives.

TIIAP. An early product of the interagency approach to the NII was the Department of Commerce's Telecommunications Information Infrastructure Assistance Program, or TIIAP, which began in 1993. An important focus of TIIAP has been the creation of "learning communities," in which schools become partners with higher education, community, business, government, and other entities.

Goals 2000. The National Education Goals were developed in 1990 through the work of the state governors and the Bush Administration under the title, America 2000. Under President Clinton they became Goals 2000, and the legislation included support for expanding the use of computers and technology in education reform. A number of states have had comprehensive statewide school improvement plans approved for funding under Goals 2000.

Improving America's Schools. As part of the 1994 Improving America's Schools Act, which amended the Elementary and Secondary Education Act of 1965, the Dwight D. Eisenhower Professional Development Program was created to upgrade teacher skills in core academic subjects set out in state content standards, using distance learning and other methods.

Technology Literacy Challenge. In February 1996 the Clinton Administration announced a Technology Literacy Challenge for the 21st Century, based on the "four pillars" of teacher training, effective learning media, and universal classroom access to multimedia computers and to the information superhighway.

21st Century Community Learning Centers. A program was established by Congress in 1997 to award grants, beginning in 1998, to rural and inner-city public schools. These grants support school-based community learning centers that offer services that may include use of advanced technology, particularly by children who do not have access to computers or telecommunications at home.

E-Rate for Universal Service. The E-Rate policy, adopted by the FCC in May 1997 for calendar year 1998 implementation, awards telecommunications services discounts of 20% to 90% to qualifying schools nationwide.

Technical Assistance

Federal support of distance education, electronic networking, and other technology use in schools includes six Regional Technology in Education Consortia (RTECs). The RTECs, funded under the Technology for Education Act of 1994, were created in 1995 to assist education institutions in effectively using advanced technologies to support improved teaching and student achievement.

Currently, the federally supported technical assistance centers (TACs) play a limited role in the school improvement process. Much of the assistance they provide focuses on compliance with regulations for states and schools receiving federal funding. The long-term, sustained assistance needed for systemic education reform is beyond their capacities. Sustained assistance also is limited by the fact that the TACs have no leverage to require schools to build local capacity for reform work (Haslam and Turnbull 1996).

Faced with limited resources, federal technical assistance centers have turned heavily to use of technology. Video conferences, web-based publications, chat groups, list servers, and other methods supplement traditional in-person seminars, meetings, and telephone and mail contact. The RTECs seek to provide the large majority of their assistance in this manner. To the extent that state and school administrators heavily adopted the use of new technologies in their work and in school reform, this strategy stands a reasonable chance of success. However, it still does not address the issue of sustained, intensive assistance. If this is to be left to the states, then they cannot succeed by simply duplicating the new federal model.

Planning and Policy Making

Following arc general recommendations that we hope will stimulate meaningful dialogue about policy making in the area of distance education and electronic networking. For convenience, we have tried to arrange the items topically, though our list is by no means comprehensive.

Written policies. A number of issues need to be addressed in written policies at the district level, school level, or through a combined effort. Barker (1991) suggests that a single policy for students in distance education courses be established and enforced. An acceptable use policy for computer labs, the Internet, and video network facilities should be established prior to operation. And a policy about the fair use of copyrighted materials by teachers, school media personnel, and students should be established to guide teachers in preparing for distance education activities. This last policy should address network use and software piracy. Specific physical and data security plans should be developed by district and school staff.

Training. Budgeting time and resources for staff technology training is critical to success. Teacher training should include both general technology skills and integration of technology in the curriculum. Student training can increase learning effectiveness and lessen supervision costs and should not be neglected. Coordinating training efforts with training opportunities offered by state, regional, or program providers can be helpful.

Evaluation. Evaluation of technology integration in learning and progress toward meeting education reform standards can be complex and time-consuming. It is critical for schools to budget adequate time and resources for evaluation. Regional and state education agencies may be able to provide resources for authentic evaluation using multiple measures to document technology use in education reform.

Facilitation and supervision. Facilitator training is necessary for many distance courses. Local staff must budget time for local tasks in relation to the distance program, including local activities specified as part of the distance course. In distance education, where the student is separated from the primary instructor, a school staff member (either a professional or an aide) should be responsible for the direct supervision of students. Some states have laws or administrative rules that require teacher certification or a special training course for aides.

Coordination and support. Those who embark on distance education need to plan on making time to deal specifically with often complicated scheduling processes. This can require extensive work with other schools to build trust and plan effectively for course sharing. Many schools need to consider the costs and benefits of moving some current activities accomplished by busing and travel to telecommunications-based modes.

Computers and printers need occasional maintenance attention, and so do television monitors and other video equipment. Identifying the local repair option and providing a budget to cover problems will reduce the potential downtime in cases of component failure. The school also should keep back-up components to replace those that can fail.

Arrangements for prompt and reliable materials transfer between students and remote teachers also are needed. Methods may include the mail, physical delivery by staff, and use of the fax and Internet. Consideration should be given to a travel budget in relation to student, facilitator, or faculty travel. Remote-site visits by teachers or by students to the originating site are common.

Facilities. There are numerous facilities issues that can affect sustained and effective use of distance education and electronic networking. Adequate space is needed for the number of students and the amount of equipment involved. Electric outlets and sufficient electrical capacity are needed for the TVs, VCRs, computers, servers, printers, fax machines, and so on.

Multimedia computers and distance education equipment also require temperature control. Air conditioning may be necessary in certain rooms, for example. In addition, the room's lighting must be controllable so that it can be used both for desk work and for using electronic equipment effectively. Room locks, equipment cabling, and locked equipment closets should be considered to protect the school's investment in technology. And, in some cases, additional soundproofing may be needed.

Planning Strategies

Planning, like policy making, requires careful attention. Following are suggested strategies (adapted from Baule 1997) that can be generalized to planning for distance education and electronic networking.

- Clearly define educational goals and objectives, current and future, and decide if technology can help meet these goals over time.
- Involve key stakeholders in the community as "sponsors" of the planning process.
- Establish a school technology committee, assess school resources and study issues.
- Identify technology champions — planning and implementation allies.
- Develop a comprehensive technology plan, including student outcomes, timelines, evaluation. (This is the time to consider policies that can assist in the development effort.)
- Create a process to involve the community in this planning effort.
- Visit other sites, explore external resource sharing and collaborative activities.

Partnering Strategies

Distance education and electronic networking are capital-intensive. Many schools and districts need financial assistance in order to reach their technology dreams. Apple Computer offers a good general strategy for successful business and community partnerships (cited in Palazzo 1995):

- Get started in-house. Create a planning team to define goals. Think about current and future relationships with businesses and brainstorm project ideas.
- Create a preliminary plan. Choose two or three projects and write an overview, description, timeline, and list of resources for each.
- Find partners. Look for local businesses, civic organizations, and cultural groups. Find out potential partners' needs. Then match projects with partners.
- Write the proposal. Tailor the plan for specific partners.
- Present the plan and follow up. Meet face-to-face with those who have the authority to accept — and fund — the proposal.
- Build a joint plan. Set measurable objectives, list specific tasks, and define resource requirements. Decide how to monitor implementation and evaluate the effect of the program.
- Implement and evaluate. Begin with a kick-off event aimed at raising awareness and building support for the project. Develop regular progress reports and periodic reviews.

- Keep the vision alive. Maintain community visibility for the project through newsletters, questionnaires, and tours. Keep communication lines open with your partners.

Working with Regional Consortia

Fenwick (1996) offers guidelines applicable to working with multidistrict and regional distance education consortia:

- Open Dialogue: Establish an atmosphere where frequent and open dialogue is expected and where appreciation of others' points of view, not consensus, is the focus. Work at discovering and listening to partisan district interests and concerns related to the consortium.
- Leadership: Appoint a full-time consortium leader, if possible, or at least a half-time leader. Grant the leader meaningful authority and reasonable independence to facilitate effective decision making.
- Agreement: Develop, with involvement of all administrators, a clear and specific consortium agreement that spells out financial arrangements, policies, and operational procedures. Communicate the details of the agreement clearly to all staff involved.
- Roles: Develop clear role descriptions to guide consistent expectations and working conditions for new staff responsibilities created by the consortium.

- Support: Provide support (including information, timely assistance, and encouragement) for staff, especially teachers, undergoing role modifications produced by the consortium.
- Delegation: Delegate authority for local decision-making to principals and help administrators adjust to new operations and management structures resulting from consortium involvement.
- Budget: Budget for extra personnel and staff time required to cope with the increased workloads produced by consortium operation.

Working with Vendors, Contractors, and Consultants

Contracting services in relation to distance education and electronic networking can be time-consuming and expensive. Strategies for maintaining control of the process include:

Developing Requests for Proposals

- Ensure that a technology inventory and needs assessment have been conducted and analyzed prior to writing the RFP.
- Study technology applications that might be useful in meeting those objectives and allow for alternative technologies to meet those needs. It is useful to obtain rough estimates and descriptions of specific systems that might meet the indicated need from several technology vendors, prior to writing the RFP.

- Consult with appropriate state and regional education agency personnel in writing the RFP, rather than relying solely on the advice of vendors. For major projects, it is best to hire a networking consultant without vendor connections to oversee RFP development or to completely develop the RFP.

Contracting

- Detail all vendor responsibilities in the contract.
- Have a school board attorney review the contract prior to signing. Obtain copies of previous contracts from references for the vendor.
- Include the timetable in the contract and, if possible, break the contract into phases with payment contingent on satisfaction.
- Address how cost overruns will be handled in the contract. Examine cost-effective alternatives, hidden costs, and possible future applications in contracting with the vendor.

Working with Contractors

- Whenever feasible, use one vendor for installation, testing, and maintenance of a network or equipment.
- Select a staff member who is knowledgeable about technology to act as the single point of contact for the school with vendors, contractors, and consultants.
- Educate the vendors, contractors, and consultants about school processes and politics that might impinge on perceptions of the technology project. Early on, involve in work with contractors all staff

who will be involved in technology maintenance, security, and related issues.

- Inform vendors and contractors about regulated issues, such as technology standards, and state wiring standards, safety and fire code regulations, and asbestos abatement.

Keeping Costs Down

- Adopt the Star network design, with a single district hub, so that schools can share network costs.
- Share resources between multiple networks.
- Coordinate purchasing at the state level, and negotiate volume discounts at the district or state level.
- Take advantage of free industry services and special programs for schools.

We hope these suggestions can help schools and school districts develop distance education and electronic networking capabilities. The Resources section of this fastback also may give educators starting points for research and development in this area.

Resources

Here are some additional sources of information that may be useful to administrators involved in making policy.

Printed Resources

Barron, A.E., and Orwig, G.W. *New Technologies for Education: A Beginner's Guide*. 3rd. ed. Englewood, Colo.: Libraries Unlimited, 1997.

This book offers an updated look at the technologies affecting education, including the World Wide Web, wireless local area networks (LANs), multimedia, and videoconferencing. Available from Libraries Unlimited, P.O. Box 6633, Englewood, CO 80155-6633.

Beckner, W., and Barker, B.O. *Technology in Rural Education*. Fastback 366. Bloomington, Ind.: Phi Delta Kappa Educational Foundation, 1994. ERIC Number ED 369 586.

Details the use of educational technology in rural schools to maximize their natural advantages and to address challenges to educational improvement. Describes technologies for schools and their libraries and evaluation of technology use. Available from Phi Delta Kappa, P.O. Box 789, Bloomington, IN 47402-0789. 800-766-1156.

CEO Forum on Education and Technology. *From Pillars to Progress: Integrating Education & Technology*. Washington, D.C., 1997.

In this, its first report on progress on the "four pillars" for technology literacy in the 21st century, the CEO Forum reported that while 3% of American schools are effectively using technology in the classroom, 60% have inadequate, outdated technology. The report is available on the web at: www.ceoforum.org. Copies can be obtained from the CEO Forum at (202) 393-1010.

Coley, R.J.; Cradler, J.; and Engel, K.P. *Computers and Classrooms: The Status of Technology in U.S. Schools*. Princeton, N.J.: Educational Testing Service, 1997.

This report from the ETS Policy Information Center reviews several recent federal and private national surveys. It examines such issues as levels and kinds of technology in schools, connecting teachers and technology, the educational impact of technology, the quality of courseware, and the costs of deploying technology in schools. Available from: Educational Testing Service Policy Information Center, Princeton, NJ 08541-0001. Full text available on the web at: http://www.ets.org/research/pic/compclass.html

Heaviside, S.; Riggins, T.; and Farris, E. *Advanced Telecommunications in U.S. Public Elementary and Secondary Schools, Fall 1996. Statistics in Brief*. NCES 97-944. Washington, D.C.: National Center for Education Statistics, U.S. Department of Education, 1997.

This annual federal survey provides a national estimate of school use of distance learning and Internet, video, and computer technologies. Equity and funding issues are addressed. Full text available on the web at: www.nces.ed.gov/pubs/97944.html

Hobbs, V., and Christianson, J.S. *Virtual Classrooms: Educational Opportunity Through Two-Way Interactive Television*. Lancaster, Pa.: Technomic, 1996.

This book provides a comprehensive review of two-way interactive television (I-TV) and includes detailed guidelines, in nontechnical language, for establishing a school-based I-TV network. Available from: Technomic Publishing, 851 New Holland Ave., Box 3535, Lancaster. PA 17604-3535.

Joint Committee on Standards for Educational Evaluation. *The Program Evaluation Standards.* 2nd ed. Kalamazoo: Western Michigan University, 1994.

Widely accepted and used by education agencies at all levels for program evaluation activities. Training also is available. Available from: The Evaluation Center, Western Michigan University, Kalamazoo MI 49008-5178.

McDougald, D., and Bowie, M. *Information Services for Secondary Schools.* Greenwood Professional Guides in School Librarianship. Westport, Conn.: Greenwood, 1997. ERIC Number ED 406 984.

Helps library media specialists develop information services to integrate information access and use into a changing curriculum. Available from Greenwood Press, 88 Post Road West, P.O. Box 5007, Westport, CT 06881-5007.

Moore, M.G., and Kearsley, G.P. *Distance Education: A Systems View.* Belmont, Calif.: Wadsworth, 1996.

A comprehensive and authoritative introduction to distance education. A good resource for learning the major components of distance education and how they work together. Available from: Wadsworth Publishing Company, 10 Davis Drive, Belmont, CA 92004.

Northwest Educational Technology Consortium. *Closing the Equity Gap in Technology Access and Use: A Practical Guide for K-12 Educators.* Portland, Ore., 1997. Online and PDF versions available at: http://www.netc.org/cdrom/equity/html/index.htm

This guide provides checklists to help you assess how well your school district is meeting equity needs in educational technology. Strategies, planning steps, and sample plans also are provided.

Pelavin Research Institute. *Investing in School Technology: Strategies to Meet the Funding Challenge*. Washington, D.C.: Office of Educational Technology, U.S. Department of Education, November 1997.

Provides comprehensive strategies for school district funding of educational technology plans. A great primer on the topic. Available on the web at: http://www.ed.gov/pubs/techinvest

Simpson, C. M. *Copyright for Schools: A Practical Guide*. 2nd ed. Professional Growth Series. Worthington, Ohio: Linworth, 1997. ERIC Number ED 406 987.

This monograph presents examples of typical public school situations involving copyright issues and gives practical advice that is based on a conservative interpretation of the copyright law. One new feature is fair use guidelines for multimedia materials. Available from Linworth Publishing, 480 E. Wilson Bridge Road, Worthington, OH 43085. 800-786-5017.

Technology Infrastructure in Schools. Hot Topic. Tallahassee, Fla.: SERVE, 1996. ERIC Number ED 398 875.

This document provides overviews of issues, appropriate questions to consider, and lists of recommendations for the non-technologically-literate user involved in making decisions about technology. Available from: SERVE, Item No. HITTERS, 345 South Magnolia Drive, Suite D-23, Tallahassee, FL 32301. Online and PDF versions available at: http://www.netc.org/cdrom/serve/html/index.htm

Wishnietsky, D.H. *Internet Basics: An Educator's Guide to Traveling the Information Highway*. Bloomington, Ind.: Phi Delta Kappa Educational Foundation, 1997.

This brief guide will help the uninitiated become literate in the use of basic Internet technologies. Available from Phi Delta Kappa, P.O. Box 789, Bloomington, IN 47402-0789. 800-766-1156.

Electronic Resources

21st Century School Technology Planning Site. http://www.ncsa.uiuc.edu/idt

This website walks educators through the entire process of upgrading a school's technology — including team building, planning, and the implementation process — by use of a functional flow chart called the Infrastructure Decision Tool. Created by the University of Illinois with NCREL funding.

CLASS Home Page. http://class.unl.edu

Planned for completion in 2000 as the world's first complete online, accredited high school. CLASS stands-for Communications, Learning, and Assessment in a Student-centered System. A project of a consortium led by the University of Nebraska, CLASS already has prototype courses online.

Nancy Willard's Acceptable Use Policies. http://www.erehwon.com/k12aup

This comprehensive collection of background materials and templates, prepared by a lawyer, are one alternative for administrators seeking to develop an acceptable use policy. The author requests a fee for use, but access for comparison purposes is free. Phone: (541) 344-9125. E-mail: nwillard@ordata.com

Northwest Educational Technology Consortium. *Networking Issues in K-12 Schools*. Portland, Ore., 1997.

This CD-ROM provides awareness and basic understanding of the issues involved in planning, implementation, and using networks in K-12 schools for technology committee members and others. Available from: NETC, 101 SW Main Street, Suite 500, Portland, OR 97204-3297. Messages: 800-211-9435. E-mail: netc@nwrel.org.

References

Barker, B.O. "K-12 Distance Education in the United States: Technology Strengths, Weaknesses, and Issues." Paper presented at the First Annual Conference of the U.S. Distance Learning Association, Washington, D.C., 10-13 April 1991. ERIC Number ED 332 687.

Baule, S.M. *Technology Planning*. Professional Growth Series. Worthington, Ohio: Linworth, 1997. ERIC Number ED 406 992.

CEO Forum on Education and Technology. *From Pillars to Progress: Integrating Education & Technology*. Washington, D.C., 1997.

Clark, T.A., and Else, D. "Distance Education Policy and Iowa Schools: A Survey of Administrators." In *Encyclopedia of Distance Education Research in Iowa, Addendum 9-23*, 2nd ed. rev. Ames: Iowa Distance Education Alliance, 1998.

Coley, R.J.; Cradler, J.; and Engel, K.P. *Computers and Classrooms: The Status of Technology in U.S. Schools*. Princeton, N.J.: Educational Testing Service, 1997.

Dede, C. "The Evolution of Distance Education." *American Journal of Distance Education* 10, no. 2 (1996): 4-36.

England, R. *A Survey of State-Level Involvement in Distance Education at the Elementary and Secondary Levels*. University Park, Pa.: American Center for the Study of Distance Education, 1991. ERIC Number ED 352 009.

Fenwick, T.J. "Issues in Forming School District Consortia to Deliver Distance Education." Edmonton: University of Alberta, 1996. ERIC Number ED 399 656.

Haslam, M.B., and Turnbull, B.J. "Issues in Federal Technical Assistance Policy." *Educational Policy* 10 (June 1996): 146-71.

Heaviside, S.; Riggins, T.; and Farris, E. *Advanced Telecommunications in U.S. Public Elementary and Secondary Schools, Fall 1996. Statistics in Brief.* NCES 97-944. Washington, D.C.: National Center for Education Statistics, U.S. Department of Education, 1997.

Holznagel, D.C., and Olson, T. *A Study of Distance Education Policies in State Education Agencies*. Portland, Ore.: NWREL, 1990. ERIC Number ED 319 402.

Jones, S. *Educational Technology: K-12 Planning and Investments in the SREB States*. Atlanta: Southern Regional Education Board, 1994. ERIC Number ED 378 947.

Krebs, A. *Distance Learning Funding Sourcebook*. Dubuque, Iowa: Kendall/Hunt, 1996.

Lee, V.E.; Bryk, A.S.; and Smith, J.B. "The Organization of Effective Secondary Schools." In *Review of Research in Education*, edited by L. Darling-Hammond. Washington, D.C.: American Educational Research Association, 1993.

Levine, J. "TV in the Classroom." *Forbes*, 27 January 1997, p. 98.

Mayer, M.; Scarborough, D.; Pollard, J.S.; Stout, C.; and Gamble, C. *The State Networking Report*. Austin: Southwest Educational Development Laboratory and Texas Education Network, 1997. ERIC Number ED 409 003.

Monk, D.H. *Secondary School Enrollment and Curricular Comprehensiveness*. Ithaca, N.Y.: Cornell University, 1986. ERIC Number ED 287 628.

National Center for Education Statistics. *Advanced Telecommunications in U.S. Private Schools, K-12 Fall 1995.* NCES 97-394. Washington, D.C.: U.S. Department of Education, 1997.

Norris, D.M. *Revolutionary Strategy for the Knowledge Age.* Ann Arbor, Mich.: Society for College and University Planning, 1997.

Palazzo, A. "Grow Your Own Business Partnerships." *Electronic Learning* 15 (October 1995): 42-47.

Pelavin Research Institute. *Investing in School Technology: Strategies to Meet the Funding Challenge.* Washington, D.C.: Office of Educational Technology, U.S. Department of Education, November 1997.

Ramirez, R., and Bell, R. *Byting Back: Policies to Support the Use of Technology in Education.* Oak Brook, Ill.: NCREL, 1994. ERIC Number ED 378 941.

Spillane, J.P. "School District Matter: Local Educational Authorities and State Instructional Policy." *Educational Evaluation and Policy Analysis* 10 (March 1996): 63-87.

Van Horn, Royal. "The Virtual School." *Phi Delta Kappan* 78 (February 1997): 481-82.

Verduin, J.R., and Clark, T.A. *Distance Education: The Foundations of Effective Practice.* San Francisco: Jossey-Bass, 1991.

Phi Delta Kappa Educational Foundation

The Phi Delta Kappa Educational Foundation was established on 13 October 1966 with the signing, by Dr. George H. Reavis, of the irrevocable trust agreement creating the Phi Delta Kappa Educational Foundation Trust.

George H. Reavis (1883-1970) entered the education profession after graduating from Warrensburg Missouri State Teachers College in 1906 and the University of Missouri in 1911. He went on to earn an M.A. and a Ph.D. at Columbia University. Dr. Reavis served as Assistant Superintendent of Schools in Maryland and Dean of the College of Arts and Sciences and the School of Education at the University of Pittsburgh. In 1929 he was appointed director of instruction for the Ohio State Department of Education. But it was as assistant superintendent for curriculum and instruction in the Cincinnati public schools (1939-48) that he rose to national prominence.

Dr. Reavis' dream for the Educational Foundation was to make it possible for educators to write and publish the wisdom they acquired through professional activity. He wanted educators and the general public to "better understand the nature of the educative process and the relation of education to human welfare."

The Phi Delta Kappa fastbacks, along with monographs and books on a wide range of topics related to education, are the realization of that dream.

Phi Delta Kappa Fastbacks

This annual series, published each fall and spring, offers fastbacks on a wide range of topics in education. Each fastback is intended to be a focused, authoritative treatment of a topic of current interest to educators and other readers. More than 400 fastbacks have been published since the program began in 1972, many of which are still in print. Topics include:

Administration
Adult Education
The Arts
At-Risk Students
Careers
Censorship
Community Involvement
Computers
Curriculum
Decision Making
Dropout Prevention
Foreign Study
Gifted and Talented
Legal Issues
Mainstreaming
Multiculturalism
Nutrition
Parent Involvement
School Choice
School Safety
Special Education
Staff Development
Teacher Training
Teaching Methods
Urban Education
Values
Vocational Education
Writing

For a current list of available fastbacks and other publications, please contact Phi Delta Kappa International, 408 North Union, P.O. Box 789, Bloomington, IN 47402-0789, or (812) 339-1156.

ISBN 0-87367-641-6

9 780873 676410